Make Money Blogging:

The Realist's Guide to Blogging for a Living

Brendan Mace

FREE BONUS: Simple Two Step Formula

Click Here to Get Your FREE Bonus

Table of Contents

Introduction

Chapter 1 -- Getting Started with Blogging

Chapter 2 -- Pick a Passion with a Commercial Audience

Chapter 3 -- Your Blogging Purpose to the Reader

Chapter 4 -- Your Site's Design and Layout

Chapter 5 -- What to Write in Your Blog Posts

Chapter 6 -- How to Get Traffic to Your Blog

Chapter 7 -- Other Way to Get Extra Traffic

Chapter 8 -- Building an Email List

Chapter 9 -- Why Site Speed Matters

Chapter 10 -- Benefits of Passive Income

Chapter 11 -- Not a Goodbye: Ask Me Anything

Introduction

The first step to **making money blogging** is to stop searching for "how to make money with blogging." Not because blogging for a living is impossible -- it is a reality for many.

The problem is the stuff you find will mostly 'lose' you money. Kind of like asking a casino owner how to make money in Vegas.

Blogging for money is not a hobby. Every guy and his grandma have created a casual blog. The audience for most of these sites extends to family and friend. If they're unlucky, maybe a handful of straggling strangers, stumbling from an obscure Google search, too.

This illusion of making easy money blogging is emboldened by the relatively few examples of bloggers that make six-figures and beyond.

... Or is it an illusion?

Most realists will tell you that blogging cannot make you money. These same people are aware that blogging can make *someone* very wealthy. After all, they have probably read a six-figure blog or two in the past twelve months. They just don't think **you** can do it.

They want you to be realistic like them.

My goal with this guide is to convince a realist to see the sheer potential of blogging for a living. Not only is it possible, but also if you take the right action as outlined here, making money from blogging is inevitable.

Don't let small minds convince you that your dreams are too big.

Grow your mind, instead.

Chapter 1 -- Getting Started with Blogging

Before cashing any checks, you need a virtual stomping ground.

A website you can call your own.

One of the biggest mistakes newbies make is they choose a free platform.

That's okay if you want a hobby blog.

And I actually show you how to do the hobby blog set up, right here.

If you're serious about blogging, though, you need a self-hosted solution.

How to Set Up Your Website

You'll WASTE years of passive income, if you don't create a website today.

Dead serious.

The #1 mistake in this industry is putting off building your own site.

Hate to be the bringer of bad news. That's the reality.

... Please don't shoot the messenger!

The **GOOD NEWS** is that creating a website is easy.

There are loads of options. Lots of freebie tools. And editors so easy, your grandma could use them.

Where Should You Start?

The first step is to register a domain name.

My personal favourite website for domains is NameSilo.com (no affiliation)

Another alternative is www.namecheap.com

For this tutorial, we're going to be working with NameSilo.

Go to this website, and set up an account. (2 mins approx)

Step #2 is finding a domain name.

If you're struggling with this take a look at LongTailPro.

It's a keyword tool that makes it easy to find keywords that get lots of searches.

However, I do not recommend picking a domain name based on the keyword. The idea here is to find a site topic that will have lots of search potential.

Nobody wants to create an entire site, and then find out that nobody cares.

Which is the reality that many of us run into with niche sites.

It may even be worth your while to dive in to an industry.

A site based on:

- Make Money Online
- Health
- Fitness

Is never going to struggle for potential viewers or customers.

The challenge is to get these eyeballs to YOUR site.

We'll cover this later...

For now, head to NameSilo.com and use the Domain finder tool and pick something.

Here's what it'll look like:

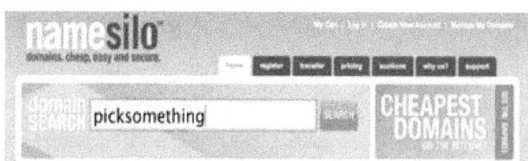

You can find this tool right at the homepage.

Very easy to use.

Once you search for a domain name, it'll take you to the next page.

Here's what you'll see:

In this case, I chose to search for "picksomething"

The tool is now telling me that:

- picksomething.com
- picksomething.net

But... **PickSomething.org** is still available.

This is where you should make a judgment call.

There is no SEO benefit for having a ".com" website.

There might be branding benefits, though, to having a ".com" domain extension. So I completely understand when people **NEED TO HAVE** a site with a com ending.

In my case, I like having a ".com" or a ".net"

So I'm going to pick something else.

Instead, I've decided on SimpleToBuild.net

That's the domain we'll be working with for the remainder of this action guide.

Step #3 is Getting Hosting for your Domain

Trust me - there's no way around this one.

Yes, you can get a free site set up with Blogger, Wix, Weebly, etc.

But let me ask you this...

Have you seen **anyone** make good money from a free website?

I've been online since 2005, and I've yet to see anybody do it.

Hosting your site is going to cost you about five bucks per month. If you can't do that, I question your dedication or any intention to actually make this work.

You need hosting - get it!

But where?

My favourite place to get hosting is from HostGator

Don't buy it yet!!

Seriously.

First you want an explanation for why to pick them as a host. And then I have a nice HostGator **coupon code** that'll save you a good slice off the final bill.

When I started online in 2005, I tried many different hosting services.

From everything I tried, HostGator was the best:

1. For site speed
2. Up time (almost never down)
3. Overall reliability

Another really good touch is that HostGator support is world class.

They respond nearly instantly, and really help solve any issues.

Having that support could be CRUCIAL if something happens to one of your sites.

And you have to imagine, an issue will probably come up at some point.

HostGator will deal with it for you.

What's the coupon code?

The coupon: **get25offyourbill**

Copy that code, and get ready to use it pretty quick.

First, sign up to a hosting plan on the homepage:

I usually recommend the "Baby Plan"

The Hatchling Plan is too limited. And the Business Plan is unnecessary.

You'll just need to fill out some basic information, and then check off some boxes.

In the next section, they'll ask you about "additional services"

It looks like this:

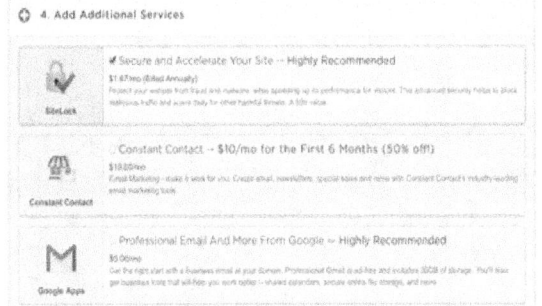

Never fear - you don't need any of these add-ons.

Uncheck all the boxes and move to the coupon section.

Now you can throw in your **coupon code** and save 25%

Looks like this:

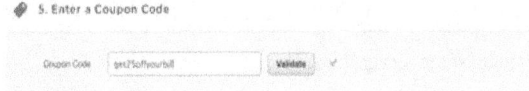

And boom.

That's it.

You now have website hosting.

You're only a couple minutes away from having your own site up and running online.

The LAUNCH - Connecting Your Domain to Hosting

At this point, we have purchased two separate services.

We bought a Domain Name + Web Hosting

Our next step is to connect these two services together.

Log in to NameSilo

Then click on the "Domain Manager" button.

You can find that on the right sidebar.

That will take you to a page with a list of your domains.

My looks like this:

Notice that most of these domains are **hosted with HostGator**.

If you pick the Baby Plan, you are allowed to have unlimited sites. So go crazy.

I recommend focusing on one site at a time. But it's really easy to add more sites to your hosting. And it won't cost you a single extra penny. Unlimited is included in your package.

Do you see those boxes on the left side of each domain?

Click on the box that's associated with the website you want to host.

For you - it'll be easy. You probably have only one site right now.

Then you just want to click on the "Change Name servers" button.

It's right above your domain list. Here:

See it between "Renew Domains" and "Park Domains?"

Exactly.

Clicking on that button will take you to this page:

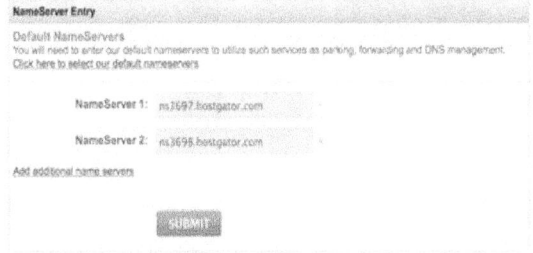

NameServer Entry

Default NameServers
You will need to enter our default nameservers to utilize such services as parking, forwarding and DNS management.
Click here to select our default nameservers

NameServer 1: ns3697.hostgator.com

NameServer 2: ns3698.hostgator.com

Add additional name servers

SUBMIT

Just enter in your name servers, and everything will be smooth sailing.

Where the heck are your name servers?

Good question!

You can find your name servers in the Welcome Email from HostGator.

After you buy your web hosting, HostGator will send you this information instantly.

It'll look like this:

1st Nameserver: ns3697.hostgator.com
2nd Nameserver: ns3698.hostgator.com
Server IP: 184.173.250.156

See how those name servers match up with my NameSilo account.

That's how I connect the two services together.

There's just one more step, and then we'll start our new Wordpress site.

We need to add the domain to our HostGator C-Panel.

This is easy.

In your control panel, scroll down to the "Domains" section.

You want to click on "Add-On Domains"

Right here:

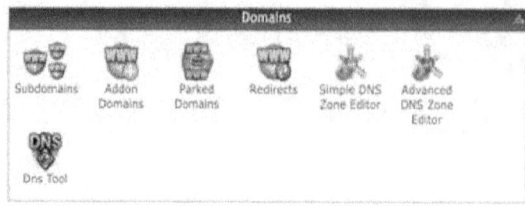

Click on that Add-on button.

Remember, you have to scroll down to find this section. If you don't see it, then you're either:

1. Not in your c-panel
2. Not scrolled down the page

The important part is that you enter the domain you just registered.

It'll look like this:

And there you have it.

A domain that's 100% connected to your hosting.

What's next?

Click on the "Get Started with Wordpress" button at the top of your HostGator C-Panel

Looks like this:

Follow a few easy steps, and you'll have a Wordpress site you can call your own.

That's it.

Congratulations!!! You have a website!

Chapter 2 -- Pick a Passion with a Commercial Audience

Sounds like we're slipping into the hobby category here, but having a passionate interest in your blog are paramount to your success.

If you don't like your topic, you won't last for the long term.

You can fake an interest for a post or two. Maybe even a dozen.

To create a lucrative blog, you need years of posting the goods. With something that disinterests you, the content will burn out. Either altogether, or the apathy towards the subject will show in your writing.

Pick something that you like writing about.

Myself, for example, could ramble about "blogging" or "making money online" for days. I wouldn't stop, even if I became a billionaire tomorrow. It's what I enjoy doing.

Don't think of it as something you "could do," instead think of what you "have to do."

What about the Commercial Audience Part?

It would be nice if we could just stop at passion, right?

You'd be free to write about your favourite bag of Doritos, or the tasty Vietnamese restaurant down the road.

Blogging for money doesn't work that way. Where there's a passion, money often follows. But that's not always the case.

Some topics don't make bloggers enough sales to be worthwhile.

There are only really two things we need to worry about here:

1. Is the Audience Big Enough?
2. Does the Audience spend money?

Many will argue with me here, and say you also need to check the competition.

Logic being that if a topic like "make money online" is too competitive, you won't be able to muster enough attention to your blog.

I disagree. If a market has lots of competition, it's usually because there's money to be made.

You can get traffic in a competitive market. It will be harder, but worth it in the end.

For this, I like to lean on the wisdom of the former **Richest Man in the World.**

"In Business, I look for economic castles protected by unbreachable moats."

- Warren Buffet

If you're in a competitive marketplace, you just need to build a castle.

When you do that, you'll have a business that's sustainable and profitable.

Is your Passion Big Enough?

My advice would be, if you have to question it -- probably not.

The bloggers that make the big bucks are mostly in these industries:

- Make money online
- Health
- Fitness
- Finance
- Stock Market
- Fashion
- Celebrities
- Food
- Gaming(?)

That's a start.

You can probably find a half dozen more that are big enough to justify blogging for money.

What about smaller niches?

Here's the thing...

You absolutely could dominate a small niche. It would take some elbow grease, some time and some dedication to your niche audience. Even then, it would not be a guaranteed earner for you.

Let's say that you're interested in bowling. You could become one of the "bowling guys" in blogging. And yes, you would make a nice "side income."

However, it would actually be more difficult to make full-time income with bowling than it would in the fitness industry. Even though it's easier to become a bigger player in the bowling industry.

That make sense?

In the big industries, you can feast more on a much smaller sliver of the pie. If you pick a small blogging niche, you could eat the whole damn pie, and still be left hungry for more.

So find the middle ground that works for you.

I picked "make money online" when I started because it was the best financial choice. It also, fortunately for me, turned into a major passion of mine.

Chapter 3 -- Your Blogging Purpose to the Reader

Your goal is probably a financial one.

When I started, my goal was to make my first $1 online.

Then my next goal was to reach $100/month. And the numbers continued to rise, until at the point of writing this, I make around $10,000 every month.

But **FORGET ALL THAT!**

Nobody cares about *your goal*.

The reader wants to know what's in it for them.

You need a ***Blogging Purpose***

This is a little tricky, because you don't want to just look like everyone else.

That's boring, and it's not going to build you a readership.

Instead, you want to stand out from the pack. You do this by having a USP (unique selling point).

A ***Unique Selling Point*** is the reason why a reader picks you.

For example, Pizza Hut is famous for selling a stuffed crust pizza. Cheese addicts will often select Pizza Hut because their *stuffed crust* has captured their main interest.

In this case, we're talking about the Pizza Restaurant industry. Pizza Hut is the business, and a stuffed crust is their unique selling point.

Does that make sense?

The Three USP's on My Blog

I'll use my blog as an example.

On BrendanMace.com, there are three things I use to distinguish my brand from the pack.

1. There's a mugshot of my face on the home page.
2. I talk about travelling -- a lot.
3. I'm transparent about pretty much everything.

For a little context, my blog is about "making money online"

That should help a little. It's not about finding something that's original to everything on the Internet. You'd expect a travel blog to talk about travelling, for instance.

A USP has to do with your particular industry. A good USP differentiates your blog from your competitors, and builds you readership.

A typical "make money online" blog is horrendous (in my opinion).

They usually have banner ads on the side, in the header of the blog, and even scattered throughout the post-copy.

Jamming ads is attractive because you can make some quick cash from an occasional sale.

You can make 10-20X more, however, by using the same "ad space" to sell yourself instead.

The mugshot of my face is different. It *intentionally* makes readers feel like they are reading from a real person. Of course, most blogs have a human writer involved. But it's easy to forget that, when half the page is packed with offers.

This is what I do, here:

Very simple, but stands out.

What could you do to make your blog more personal?

Simple little touches that add your personality go a long way. Your business is about developing connections with your readers. Do that -- and making cash will be easy.

The Travelling Rambles -- Why?

Another USP on BrendanMace.com is the constant 'travel talk.

Why?

My blog is about **"making money online**." It may seem like a giant waste of words to focus on something that doesn't make money online, but it gives me a unique selling point.

There are loads of bloggers that brag about their numbers. Showing statistics about the amount of visitors they get per month, and how much net profit they make while sleeping in their mansions. And heck, I do some of this too (minus the mansion). But not many "make money online" bloggers talk about travelling.

To me, travelling is more down to earth. It's something many every-day guy or gal wants to do, but usually has a reason not to.

You may be thinking at this point, "I don't want to travel. I could care less about anything outside my basement."

And to that, I would say, "are you out of your fucking mind?"

Just kidding. Sort of...

The point I actually want to make is that you shouldn't try and please everyone. It's impossible, and you're more likely to be left with nobody.

The much better option is to build a tribe. To stand out, and grow a group of readers that are obsessed with your USP(s).

Full Transparency USP -- Industry specific

The last of my three USP's is transparency.

This would not be unique in other industries, like fitness or gaming.

When it comes to "make money online," however, most bloggers don't freely talk about their income sources, which is weird.

Keeping your hand hidden is the norm for Internet marketing.

For the clever bloggers out there, this unusual behavior is a welcome opportunity.

Any industry with lopsided norms is ripe for a **pattern interrupt.**

A "pattern interrupt" is an attention tsunami. Not everyone is going to like your interruption, but almost everyone will notice it.

Matthew Woodward -- A blogging Interrupter

Matthew Woodward has one of the coolest blogs in marketing.

His site clears 6-figures per year, and packs a blogging punch of awesomeness.

Matthew's most famous for his SEO (search engine optimization) ability. Which in layman's terms means his aptitude for ranking websites in search engines like Google.

When he started his blog, the blogging purpose was a "no back link experiment." Which means that he intended to demonstrate how to rank a website without building any backlinks.

The pattern for "website rankers" was to abuse backlinks. A typical blogger in that space would have experiments about how a certain 'link' affects a site's rankings.

It was unusual, for Matthew, to create an SEO focused blog that intentionally avoids backlinks.

That's like a world-class chef claiming he can make you a delicious meal without any food.

He did it, though. And his blog thrived because he chose to do something different.

How Do You Add a USP to Your Blog?

1. Brainstorm the norms in your market
2. Brainstorm what you could do differently
3. Pick at least one USP, and brand the crap out of it

Just be careful. Don't be different for the sake of difference.

Nobody is showing their genitals while blogging about mashed potatoes.

Sometimes nobody is doing something for a good reason.

Use your common sense to decide whether _your difference_, will give your blog the right purpose to move forward.

Chapter 4 -- Your Site's Design and Layout

First of all, you need a logo.

Without one, you will not build a brand. And you will not look different.

My favourite spot for logo designs is a site called Fiverr.com

This site hosts a marketplace of freelancers that are willing to do small tasks for $5.

You can get anything from written articles to a drunken impersonation of Marilyn Monroe singing Happy Birthday. Lots of stuff. And everything is on the cheap.

If you're not careful, you can drop over $100 on random Fiverr gigs, though.

Cheap over time can really add up.

Here's my site's logo:

Simple, classy and gets my USP across.

My blog is about building a laptop business from a beach.

This logo captures that message, and it's not obnoxious about it.

Where did I get this awesome logo?

... You guessed it. On Fiverr.com for five buckaroos.

Here's the seller I bought from:

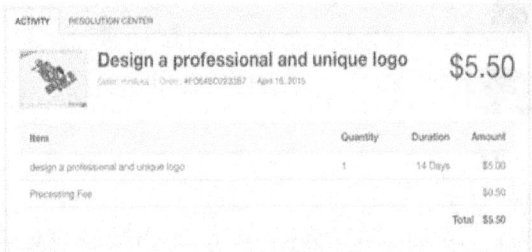

Awesome deal!

There's a bunch of logo designers on Fiverr.

Check it out, and save yourself the hassle of designing it yourself.

Using a Wordpress Theme to Shortcut the Look and Feel

In the past, if you wanted a "cool" looking blog, you'd either need professional web-designer skills, or you'd need to dish out thousands of dollars to have the design done for you.

That sucks.

Now you can get a professional blog design for less than 100 bucks. And I still see blog owners bitch and complain about dropping a little cash on a quality Wordpress theme.

That's a whole bowl of shortsightedness. These "Negative Nancy's" plan on making $1k+/month from their blog, but they can't drop $100 to get the right 'look and feel' for their website.

There are many bloggers that have split tested different designs and layouts. The income difference from one to the next is often massive.

Trust me, getting a quality look is one of the best investments in the business.

The Wordpress Themes I Recommend

You really cannot go wrong with StudioPress Themes.

This company has put together a smorgasbord of various Wordpress themes, so that you can find the exact one that fits your blogging needs.

The theme used on BrendanMace.com is called MagazinePro

You can see it here:

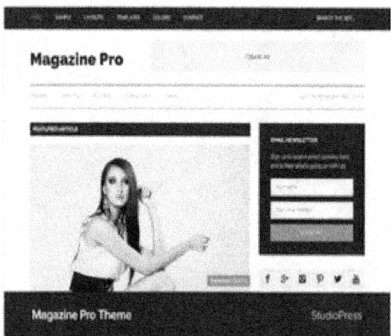

It cost me $97, which may seem expensive to some. In the grand scheme of things, less than $100 on a serious business is a bargain.

Side Note: Blogging for money is a business -- not a hobby. If you opened a business on Main Street, think of all the expenses you would pay.

You'd owe rent, utilities, cost of goods, worker salaries, etc.

Just because your expenses with an online business are typically lower, that does not mean you should avoid investing at all costs.

When you have an opportunity to drop a little money to improve your business a lot -- take that opportunity.

Chapter 5 -- What to Write in Your Blog Posts

The "work" involved in blogging is the content creation.

Sure, once you have a steady online income stream, you'll be able to afford outsourcing some of this content creation, if you want to.

Until then, you will need to write this stuff yourself.

Your blogging livelihood depends on the posts you write. Understandably, this is an important problem that you will have to solve.

My recommendation is to do some keyword research.

The key here is to find out what people are searching for on Google.

The easiest and cheapest way to get (some) keyword information is to go direct to the source.

With the first easy keyword strategy, open up Google.com on your browser, and start typing in industry related words.

What we're looking for here is the "auto generated keyword suggestions."

These suggestions tell us what people are commonly looking for.

An example here shows the a simple search of "blogging f"

Right away, we can see that "blogging for beginners" and for 'money' are two very popular options.

If we were blogging on the topic "make money blogging" these would be great keywords to target.

The problem here is that blogging relies on many blog posts over time. If we just wanted a keyword or two, this autocomplete strategy would work.

However, we need more, so we need a more expansive tool.

My favourite tool for getting keywords quick and easy is LongTailPro.

You can find my **full review of it here.**

Side Note: The last couple sections both recommend spending a little money to shortcut your blogging. I promise you there is not much left to buy. However, these little investments are worth your while.

Chapter 6 -- How to Get Traffic to Your Blog

As proved by Matthew's blog, you're better off ignoring backlinks.

You may have never heard about the benefits of backlinks before. If that's the case, consider yourself lucky. The strategy of abusing backlinks for rankings is not realistic anymore.

The better option is to use <u>high quality content,</u> "*in the right way*" to get traffic.

That 'right way' part will be discussed in a moment.

The only way people are going to see your blog, is if you show it to them.

What is the Right Way to Promote Your Blog?

We know that backlinks aren't going to work, and playing the waiting game is futile.

The best option is to get our content in front of an audience.

There are a few ways to do that, but in this guide, I'm going to feature my favourite three.

The Biggest Myth of Blog Traffic

In the blogging sphere, there's an annoying little myth, which discourages actual progress.

This myth is that great content is enough.

Let me explain why this is untrue with an analogy.

One of my favourite movies from the 80's was **Field of Dreams**.

Just a couple weeks ago, I watched it with my girlfriend, and despite her dislike of baseball, she still thought it was a great flick.

It's often misquoted with "Build it and They Will Come"

When in actuality, it was "<u>Build it and He Will Come</u>"

While it was a feel good moment in the movie, if you treat your blog this way, you are going to get hosed.

In other words, you'll never see good traffic or Google rankings.

This is something most people don't realize. They expect people to come.

The Fantasy Unravels

There's this notion that:

If you build it, they will come.

This appeals to us because it seems like a fair deal.

You provide value and you're rewarded with TRAFFIC.

Not true!

The reality is that it's not what you write that matters...

It's how you _**MARKET**_ what you write.

You could have the best-written content in the world. It does not matter.

Who's going to see it?

How to Market Your Crap?

This is a BIG topic.

I mean _big_ in more ways than one.

**Firstly,** it's big in terms of importance.

Traffic is the oxygen of your business.

Without it - your site will die.

**Secondly,** it's discussed a lot.

Which leads to information overload. And a myriad of frustrated marketers.

There are many strategies for **getting traffic to your blog.**

The most popular two are breadcrumbs and the skyscraper technique.

In this post, we'll be looking at **my results** from the latter.

What is the Skyscraper Technique?

The concept is simple.

1. Find a blog post with TONS of social shares. Let's call this **Post X.**
2. Create something better than **Post X**. Make it longer, more visual, and more exceptional.
3. Contact the people that shared **Post X**, and show them _YOUR_ stuff.

Easy enough, right?

This leads us to a couple crucial questions.

• Where do we find these posts?
• Where do we find these sharers?

There's ONE tool that does both of these for you.

BuzzSumo (no affiliation) is a search engine that scrapes the amount of social sharers for any topic of your choice.

Here's a look for the BuzzSumo search: How to Make Money on YouTube

When you type in any search, BuzzSumo reveals what content has the most shares.

But wait...

It gets even better than that.

Clicking on **"View Sharers,"** actually shows _WHO_ shared it.

As seen here:

After clicking on "View Sharers"

...BuzzSumo will provide you with a list of the people that shared that piece of content.

Pretty cool, right?

But what the heck can I do with that?

Welcome to the Skyscraper Method

Now we can take our list of sharers, and contact them directly.

There are a number of ways to do this.

We can:

1. Tag them in a Tweet
2. Email them from their website
3. Call them on the phone

The most common way is **option #2**

It also happens to be quite easy to do.

We go to their website, and then we find their "contact us" page.

Not all websites have these - but the good one's will.

Then we send them a message.

Here's where it ***gets a little dicey...***

When you contact potential sharers of your blog, you have a couple ways to go.

You could bluntly ask them to share your stuff. This will have a reasonably high success rate.

BUT it will also piss off a bunch of future contacts.

I do NOT recommend this!

The better option is to just let them know about your content.

Some marketers would consider this quite passive. And in general, it's the kind of behaviour that's frowned upon in **Make Money Online.**

It stands out, though. In a good way.

Instead of being pushy, you're kindly sharing a good post with them.

We already know these contacts are willing to share stuff. That's how we found them.

With just a little nudge, we can get them to share OUR stuff.

The whole idea here is that you are finding the right people.

And showing them something you know they'll be interested in.

Now, let's look at an example...

I created a long 4,000+ post on **How to Grow a YouTube Channel.**

This post was exceptional.

It covered the whole process of how to get YouTube subscribers, and even shared a couple lesser-known tricks to steal some easy traffic. Highly recommended post.

So I wanted to test the ***Skyscraper Technique*** on this post to see what kind of results I could get with it.

So I went into my copy of BuzzSumo, and search for YouTube Marketing.

My search found some really good stuff.

Take a look:

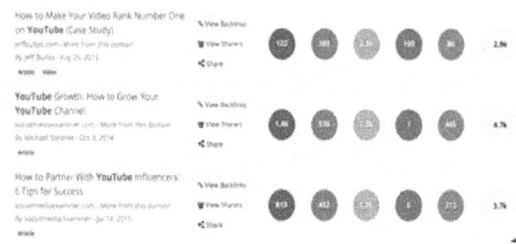

So I completed the Skyscraper Technique as discussed.

I clicked on "View Sharers"

And I started contacting these sharers one by one.

It was tedious.

I hated it.

But I started getting some results.

If you know anything about me, though, you'll know that I HATE WORK!

Seriously.

This whole blog and YouTube channel started because I didn't want a day job.

Boring tasks are the bane of my existence.

And they should be for you, too.

So I found a guy on FaceBook willing to complete these tasks for $5/hour.

Can you imagine that?

ONLY FIVE BUCKS

... FOR A FULL HOUR!!

Turns out when you find someone that lives in a county like, Thailand or the Philippines, they are very likely to work for cheap. Their cost of living is a lot lower, and consequently need a lot less money to pay their bills.

Side note: I'm off to Thailand on February 2nd.

One of the BEST advantages of the laptop lifestyle!

Anyways, so I purchased 5 hours from this dude in total.

Here's our first messages back-and-forth:

Stephen Arbole   7/12, 8:54am

Im offering you $5 an hour of service and collect fees via Paypal weekly. How was that for you?

July 12

Brendan Mace   7/12, 9:26pm

That sounds good to me. I may have a job for you.

It's basically a data-entry type job. Really easy to do. Just click add emails and click send. You could get away with listening to music while you do it.

If that's something that interests you - I'll create a video that explains the job task.

I gave him $25, and he contacted these sharers for 5 hours.

Later in this post, I'm going to reveal the results.

I also created a video, detailing the task.

This is not mandatory, but it made it easier for me to explain.

If this video would help you get someone to do this task, feel free to direct them to the below video:

Warning: I'm really sick in this video, and it's far from a good production.

But, it outlines what's expected for this task, if you plan to outsource like I did.

In my opinion, it's worthwhile to outsource any task that's boring.

Especially when people will do it of for only $5.

Moving On:

Immediately after starting this task. I started receiving email replies from a handful of sharers.

Pretty exciting stuff.

Some of the messages were from people that were downright PISSED.

Here's one:

My preference is to ALWAYS include someone's name. Instead of a term like: "buddy"

Unfortunately, Stephanie's website didn't provide her name.

Or, BuzzSumo was unable to properly scraper name information.

This stuff happens.

Don't let it ruin your day.

There was, of course, also a bunch of positive responses to my message.

Here's one of them:

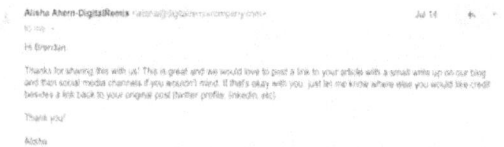

This message led to a very pleasant conversation. Both of us were able to help each other out in very constructive ways.

Booyah!

At the end of the day - how were the results?

The results were decent.

This turned out to be a worthwhile investment of $25.

But it was not a silver bullet.

There are two things that we care about the most here:

1. How many shares did I get?
2. How much money did I make?

How many shares?

I was actually hoping for more...

I ended up with these results:

How to Get 72,719 YouTube Views in the Next 30 Days (Step-By-Step)

July 12, 2015 by Brendan Mace — 8 Comments (Edit)

You get it, right?...

By 2017, Cisco estimates that **67% of web traffic** will be **video content.** Not only are videos much easier to create than long winded articles, they're also consumed with a higher retention rate.

Most people don't read . . .

- 44 Twitter shares
- 42 FaceBook shares
- 10 Google Plus Shares

For a total of 96 shares.

Not bad.

How much money did I make?

From this post launching, I can attribute TWO affiliate sales for $42 a pop.

That works out to be $84 in gross revenue from this method.

Minus $25 for outsourcing costs.

We're looking at a ***profit of $59***

Not massive. But that's free money.

I paid someone else to do the work.

And I collected the affiliate commissions.

Would I recommend this strategy?

100% I would.

As mentioned before, this is not a silver bullet.

It will not get you rich.

However, it's a good way to make some easy money while building some nice social shares at the same time.

Of course, your content needs to be very good to get these results.

My post on **Growing a YouTube Channel** was top notch.

Don't expect to throw up a junky 500-word article, and get similar results.

The people you are contacting are willing to share, but ONLY if its good stuff.

Chapter 7 -- Other Way to Get Extra Traffic

The Skyscraper Method and Guest Posting are both great ways to get traffic.

They do require a lot of work, though.

An easier way to get traffic is what I like to call the "Infiltrator Method"

The idea is simple

1. Find out where your audience hangs out
2. Add value to the conversation(s)
3. Siphon back to your blog

The best way to find your audience is to use a tagging based system.

There's a free tool called **Google Alerts,** where you'll be sent a "keyword based" notification anytime Google discovers new content that is created in your subject area.

This is a 100% free way to get more traffic.

All you need to do is monitor the notifications, and then siphon traffic back from the source Google finds.

There's a bit of a trick here, though.

It's not enough to go to these publications, and shamelessly drop your link back to your blog.

Any site with reasonable quality control will delete your link. Meaning that only the lower quality sites will even let you post that kind of garbage.

The better way to do this is to **provide value first**. Then when you drop your link, the site owner will recognize that your contribution is not entirely selfish. It's a win-win to keep you there.

It's even okay to have a "copy + paste" message written up on a topic area. And in fact, that's probably the most effective way to do it.

For example, if I use a Google Alerts for "keyword research," I have a template message already created on how to get the best results with keywords. At the end of this template message, I let people know that if they want more information, they can visit my blog for more details.

Instead of re-writing this message every time, I can use it ***any time*** that Google has a notification for "keyword research."

I may have to edit it a tiny bit to personalize it to the particular post. But overall, this copy and paste system will save me a lot of time.

Finding a Forum to Add Value

Another great opportunity is to Google search for forums in your area.

When I Google search "make money online" forums, right away I see two results:

BlackHatWorld and WarriorForum are both goldmines of potential blog readers.

Not only can you get a lot of visitors back to your blog. The traffic is generally very response.

After all, think about it. The reason why people clicked over to your site is because they like what you had to say.

This is going to be like random Google traffic that stumbles on your site.

It's going to be laser-targeted visitors that already position you as an expert.

Your user metrics for "time on site" will go through the roof. Which will indirectly help your Google rankings as well.

Talk about a powerful traffic strategy.

All you need for "Forum Marketing" is to have a good signature.

Here's mine:

Everything is in **BOLD TEXT** and encourages people to click over.

The more value you add in the forum, the more likely people will visit your site.

If you're seen as an expert on the forum -- even better.

Visitors will be flocking to your site, ready to give you their well-earned attention.

Chapter 8 -- Building an Email List

If you don't build a list, you're leaving _most_ of the money on the table.

Notice, I'm saying "most" here -- that's true.

Think about it, if you get one Google visitor, you probably have a chance to make _only one sale on that day_.

If you capture a subscriber, you can keep a loyal follower for life.

... That's _365 emails per year_ (at a rate of one per day) and a load of extra blog visits and affiliate sales.

It's pretty clear. Capturing the lead is your number one monetization strategy.

The Best Way to Convert Visitors into Subscribers

Put Email Form(s) directly on Your Site

There are lots of vacant places on your blog for an email form.

I have a few places that I recommend the most:

- On your sidebar
- On your blog header
- Before your content
- In the content
- Pop Up for Visitor Departures

You can really get creative here. If you're really a stickler for maximizing conversion rates, you could boost up your numbers by having specific forms for each specific post.

For example, a blog post about "list building" could have an email form that promises an "Email Marketing Cheat Sheet" bonus. In order to get that cheat sheet, visitors would need to subscribe to the specific web-form on that one specific blog post.

It would take a bit of extra work, but the extra opt-ins may be worth your while. I'll be honest here and say I don't do this. It takes a good amount of time, and I'd rather focus on other areas of my business.

For simplicity sake, my favourites for _on-blog_ email forms are **the sidebar**, the **pop up** and **before the content**.

My blog doesn't actually have a sidebar form. Not because it's a bad idea, I simply went in another direction.

The **Pop Up,** however, results in the largest portion of my new subscribers.

I enthusiastically encourage you to add this to your blog.

Won't a pop up bother my visitors?

Great question.

Some people will take this the wrong way -- that's an unavoidable reality for pretty much anything you create.

But really, why should anyone care?

The **Pop Up** that I use is easily closed able, which is important to me, and makes the brief pop up interruption as short as a half taken breath.

In fact, it doesn't in any way prevent visitors from leaving my site.

It activates when a visitor indicates they are about to leave, and encourages visitors to join my blog mailing list. If a visitor still decides they want to leave without subscribing, this offer in no way prevents them from doing so.

Any person that complains about a non-obstructing pop up needs to chill.

And besides, they're leaving anyways.

This is your last chance at gaining a long-term visitor to your blog. Any subscribers are a huge bonus that will provide easy traffic for any future posts.

Here's a look at my pop up:

Check out my blog, and you can see this pop up in real time.

The other place "on my blog" that collects leads on autopilot is the before content form.

This next form is a little more obstructing.

In this case, visitors see the form before they see any of your content.

To some people, this is really off-putting. Because before you even add any value, you're already asking for a favour.

While this does get subscribers, I can understand why this would prompt some people to leave your site earlier.

For that reason, I only have this form on my home page.

That way, it doesn't distract from my blog content in any significant way. And most people that really enjoy my blog content will visit the home page and see my form.

You can see my before content form here:

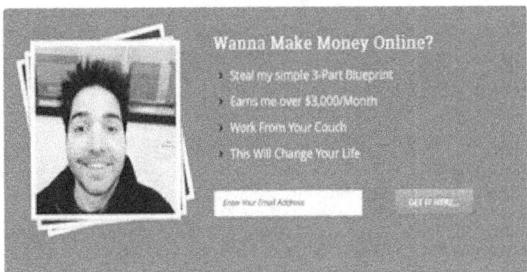

These two "on-site" forms roll in some free subscribers.

The crucial concept in this section is that blog followers via email are what separate full-time bloggers from struggling "wantrapreneurs."

A good blogger finds a way to build a returning audience.

The easiest way to do that is with an email list.

What Emails Should You Send to New Subscribers?

Your best option is to create an email series.

The service I use is **Aweber**

You can get a 30 day free trial of Aweber right here.

In your free trial of Aweber, you need to click on the "Create a Message button"

You can see this green button on the right side of your account.

Here's a look at mine:

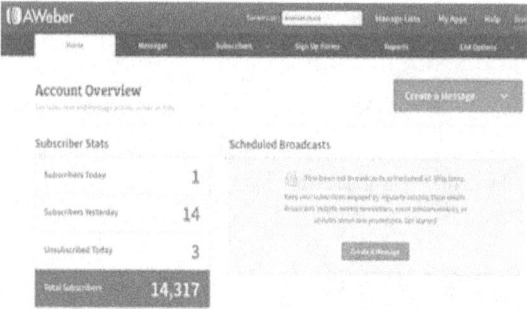

You'll then be taking to an editor.

This looks just like Microsoft Word, or whatever word processor that you're used to.

Basically, you create your emails, and then save them when you're done.

I recommend creating at least 20 emails to start, and then build over time.

Actually, my email series is over 240+ messages.

It didn't get that way overnight; I gradually keep adding more emails over time.

Don't worry, though. Emails are not like blog posts. They don't have to be long.

Just a simple, to the point message to your subscribers.

The best email conversions happen when you create personal emails. Subscribers feel like you are talking directly to them, and not like you're just blasting out to thousands of people at once.

Keep that in mind while you write your email series.

Here's a look at my first five messages in the series:

1. Booyah! YOU are now subscribed to Brendan Mace
2. Create Your Own $867.26/month Niche Site
3. Crazy NEW Keyword Method - 100% Awesome

4. 4 Easy Steps to Unlimited Traffic on Autopilot
5. Create a Profitable Niche Site in 20 Minutes or Less

Not only will email get more visitors to your blog, it will also make you sales as well.

The emails that I write serve a number of different purposes.

1-- My Coaching program

My emails often tell people about my coaching services.

In **my coaching program** I share absolutely everything I know about "making money online" and we set everything up together step-by-step.

This allows me to help many followers achieve their goals, and many actually quit their jobs.

My business only takes about 15 minutes per day to maintain, and I make enough to pay all my bills.

2-- Blog/Video Tutorials

In these emails, I direct traffic to my online tutorials. This builds a relationship with my list, gets traffic to my blog, and also helps people learn new marketing skills.

This essentially leverages the valuable content you create on your blog, and serves it up to an active and engaged audience.

3-- Affiliate Promotions

When I find a product worth recommending, I'll send an email to my subscribers letting them know about it.

These emails are delicate. You do not want to promote garbage. That will ruin your reputation faster than obnoxiously farting on a first date.

I wait for products that I actually use myself before sharing with my subscribers.

This works the same for blog or email.

Two Simple Steps:

1. Find good products
2. Promote them

Easy cash, and useful to many.

4-- Engagement Driven Emails

These are my personal favourite of the emails I send.

Their purpose is simple -- to get engagement.

An example email subject line I use is "***How Can I Help You?***"

In this email, I'm asking subscribers to contact me with whatever they need help with.

Many subscribers do take me up on this, and I fortunately get to work with many of my followers.

Some refuse to do this. After all, it takes some "_real work_" to engage directly with your subscribers.

In my opinion, it's an exceptional use of your time.

An average engagement response takes me 60 seconds or less. In most cases subscribers are asking a specific question that really only takes one or two paragraphs to answer.

In that 60 second or less timespan, I have usually created a loyal follower for life.

The subscribers I answer will see my email more often, buy more products from my recommendations, and definitely follow my blog more closely.

This is one relatively untapped area with a goldmine of value.

Do not underestimate the power of helping people directly.

Chapter 9 -- Why Site Speed Matters

One of the biggest mistakes people make is ignoring site speed.

There are two problems with having low speed.

1. It Creates a bad user experience
2. Google will hate you for it

In the mess of writing posts and promoting content, it sometimes gets forgotten to look at the overall experience.

Any user that visits a slow website is more likely to bounce, and a lot less likely to buy.

Google's disdain for slow loading times is getting even more intense.

And it makes sense for this search behemoth to care so much. Having a bad user experience is unprofessional. It may seem unfair for Google to penalize so harshly, but they are usually just looking for accurate indicators about a site's quality.

You'll get fewer visitors to a slow site, and the people you get are less likely to stay as long.

The good news is that site speed is easy to improve.

The Main Problems that Ruin Your Site Speed -- And what to do about it

A couple years ago, I had no idea how the Internet worked.

While on vacation in Cuba, I noticed that my blog was running way slower.

My first reaction was that Cuba must have terrible Internet speed.

The confusion, though, was that websites like **Google** and **FaceBook** maintained a high-speed connection.

Why Would My Blog Get the Short End of the Stick?

And then I found out.

When visiting my blog, the information from my blog's server location has to virtually travel to the location of my Internet connection.

In simpler talk, if my blog is set up in Seattle, USA, and someone opens it elsewhere, the information has to travel all the way from Seattle to that visitor's location.

That means that any person close to my hosting server will get the fastest site speeds, but most international visitors will have a much slower experience.

The easy fix for this is to use a CDN.

What is a Content Delivery Network?

A CDN is a network of servers that distributes your content delivery around the globe.

Each visitor is sent your site's information from the country on the CDN that's the closest to his or her location.

This means that regardless of whether a visitor is in South East Asia, Europe, Cuba, etc., your site will consistently deliver a faster site speed.

A good option for this is called MaxCDN (no affiliation)

This small change will dramatically improve your blog's speed for visitors around the world.

Another Important Blog Decision for Site Speed

You must know that you need a hosting service.

This will affect the site speed.

My best recommendation is to use **HostGator for budget hosting**.

There are very expensive hosting providers that deliver the fastest site speeds. The one I'm using for BrendanMace.com costs me $50/month. That's something you'll want to add as your blog grows past 10,000 visitors per month.

Until then, most hosting services are between $4-10/month.

HostGator is a very reasonable price. It costs about $5/month for the Baby Plan.

If you use the coupon code **"get25offyourbill"** you'll get an additional 25% discount off your hosting order.

Chapter 10 -- Benefits of Passive Income

Every month, I post my business results on my blog.

I call these income reports.

As of right now, I'm making around **$10,000 per month.**

The even better news is that my business really only takes about 15 minutes per day to maintain.

That means that on a low effort month, I would spend about *7.5 hours* working.

During that month, I would still make $10,000.

Which means that my income rate is approximately **$1,333.33/hour**.

That's the number after taking my income and dividing it by hours worked.

What to Do with All that Time?

Tim Ferris calls this the New Rich.

The idea being that time is an asset that's at least as valuable as money.

Under this philosophy, even a millionaire could be "time-poor," if a job prevents him from living his life.

 By working faithfully eight hours a day you may eventually get to be boss and work twelve hours a day.

It's not just about making money.

It's also about building an income stream that doesn't enslave your precious time.

To become a member of the new rich, you must build passive income.

When you do that, you'll win back your life.

What I do with My Time

In the last eight months I've traveled to:

- The Okanagan
- Vancouver

- Las Vegas
- Cuba
- Medellin
- San Andreas Island
- Panama City
- Thailand
- Cambodia
- Vietnam

Here's a view shot of the beach at Koh Tao:

To me, travelling is what keeps me sane.

It's not just about making the money that's important. It's what I do with my time that matters the most.

There are a lot people that say, "Money doesn't buy happiness"

Which is a debatable statement. You have both sides of the coin here. In my opinion, it's shortsighted to think money can't affect your life.

The truth is that money may not buy happiness, but poverty can buy a whole lot of misery.

The reason for making money blogging is to give you freedom.

We all have our reasons for wanting this.

For me, I want to be laying on a beach on my terms. And work only when I want to.

You know what the crazy thing is?

Travelling the world is not that expensive.

When you trade dollars for pesos, your money will go a lot further.

Nomadic Matt is a travel blogger.

He also wrote a book titled "How to Travel the World on $50 per Day"

That's just $1,500 per month. And that's an average of every country in the whole freaking world. You could live even cheaper if you slumber onto a beach area in South East Asia.

Do you need to travel?

Absolutely not.

But find something worth doing with your time.

For some of us, that means more time to spend with the family.

For others, that might just mean a little more down time for television and movies. Don't feel guilty about that. Many of us have been working too hard for too many years.

It's time to win your life back.

Chapter 11 -- Not a Goodbye: Ask Me Anything

"You can, you should, and if you're brave enough to start, you will"

- Steven King

I know you're busy. I know that it's more comfortable to give up.

Don't let time slip by because you're too afraid to make a change.

Building an online business was the best thing I ever did in my life. Where else can you start a business with such a low barrier to entry?

Your costs are minimal. Your obligations are non-existent.

Do this for yourself, and live your life on your terms.

The "Not a Goodbye"

Just because this guide is ending does not mean our connection is over.

If you enjoyed reading this, **sign up to my email list.**

I have coached over a hundred students. At least a dozen of which have now quit their jobs.

Almost all my students at least create a "side income"

Creating $1,000/month with blogging is very possible. It may seem unattainable now, but I promise you, once you get the ball rolling, you'll start to dream of even higher income numbers.

Ask Me Anything

I have an open invitation to connect with me.

If you need help building a business, I can get you to the next level a lot faster. And you'll be able to avoid a lot of the mistakes I made when starting out.

My last piece of advice is this: Don't let *small minds* convince you that your dreams are TOO BIG. You can do this!

If you would like to learn more about passive, then I would love to chat with you. Check out my blog that shares in depth guide, like this one. **Right here: www.BrendanMace.com**